The Shelter

by Cameron Macintosh

illustrated by Maxime Lebrun

OXFORD
UNIVERSITY PRESS
AUSTRALIA & NEW ZEALAND

It was a bright, crisp morning.

Zak, Kim and Mum were out on a sand bar when the wind started to hiss.

"I can see rain," said Zak. "We need to go back to the car."

"Oh no, we are far from the car,"
said Kim. "What can we do?"

"We can set up a little shelter," said Zak.

Mum and the children went to pick up some driftwood.

They laid the driftwood on one big log to form a shelter.

Zak, Kim and Mum went into the shelter.

"Look at the rain," said Mum.

"I can hear thunder, too," said Zak.

"Trust me, this shelter will not stop the rain," said Kim.

"Look, lightning!" said Mum. "We need to go back to the car now!"

"We will all get wet!" said Zak.

"We will not get wet under the rug," said Mum.

Mum, Zak and Kim ran back to the car.

They all got so wet!

Mum, Zak and Kim got into the car.

"I'm glad to be in the car," said Zak. "It's much better than the shelter!"